INDONESIA
TRAVEL GUIDE
2023

GIUSEPPE ROSSI

Indonesia

Travel Guide
2023

Explore the Best of Jakarta, Bali, Komodo, Flores, Papua, and More - A Comprehensive Handbook for Adventure, Culture, Beaches, and Natural Wonders in Southeast Asia's Archipelago"

By

GIUSEPPE ROSSI

Unveiling the Enchanting Charms of Indonesia: My Unforgettable Vacation in the Archipelago of Wonders

Chapter 1: Introduction to Indonesia
- Overview of Indonesia's geography and location
- Brief history and cultural diversity
- Indonesia's major cities and regions
- Climate and best time to visit
- Essential travel information and tips

Chapter 2: Exploring Jakarta
- Introduction to the capital city
- Top attractions, including the National Monument, Istiqlal Mosque, and National Museum
- Cultural experiences in Jakarta, such as visiting Kota Tua and exploring its museums
- Shopping and dining recommendations
- Practical information for navigating the city

Chapter 3: Bali: The Island of Gods
- Introduction to Bali and its significance in Indonesian culture
- Popular beach destinations, such as Kuta, Seminyak, and Nusa Dua
- Ubud: The cultural heart of Bali
- Temples and religious sites, including Besakih Temple and Uluwatu Temple

- Adventure activities, such as surfing, diving, and hiking
- Balinese cuisine and traditional dance performances

Chapter 4: Yogyakarta and Central Java
- Discovering Yogyakarta's rich history and heritage
- Exploring Borobudur Temple, Prambanan Temple, and other UNESCO World Heritage Sites
- The Sultan's Palace (Kraton) and Water Castle (Taman Sari)
- Traditional arts and crafts, including batik and wayang kulit
- Mount Merapi and outdoor adventures

Chapter 5: Exploring the Magnificent Komodo Islands
- Introduction to Komodo National Park and its unique wildlife
- Komodo dragon encounters and guided tours
- Snorkeling and diving in crystal-clear waters
- Padar Island and its stunning viewpoints
- Exploring the local villages and experiencing Komodo culture

Chapter 6: The Cultural Treasures of Sumatra
- Introduction to Sumatra's diverse cultures and landscapes

4

- Visiting the orangutan sanctuaries in Bukit Lawang and Ketambe
- Exploring the UNESCO-listed sites of Samosir Island and Gunung Leuser National Park
- Lake Toba and the Batak culture
- Traditional dances, music, and culinary delights

Chapter 7: Eastern Indonesia: Flores and Beyond
- Discovering the unique landscapes of Flores Island
- Wae Rebo Village and its traditional cone-shaped houses
- Kelimutu National Park and its three-colored lakes
- Diving in the pristine waters of Komodo National Park
- Lesser-known islands, such as Sumba, Alor, and Raja Ampat

Chapter 8: The Natural Wonders of Papua
- Introduction to Papua's breathtaking natural beauty
- Raja Ampat Islands and its world-class diving spots
- Exploring the Baliem Valley and witnessing traditional Dani tribe culture
- Climbing Puncak Jaya, the highest peak in Indonesia

- Wildlife encounters, including birdwatching and orangutan spotting

Chapter 9: Practical Information and Travel Tips
- Visa requirements and entry regulations
- Health and safety advice for travelers
- Transportation options within Indonesia
- Money and budgeting tips
- Cultural etiquette and do's and don'ts
- Useful phrases in Bahasa Indonesia

Chapter 10: Sample Itineraries
- One week in Bali: Highlights and must-see attractions
- Two weeks in Java: Exploring Jakarta, Yogyakarta, and Mount Bromo
- Off-the-beaten-path adventure: Flores, Komodo, and Raja Ampat
- Family-friendly trip: Bali and Lombok
- Nature and wildlife-focused itinerary: Sumatra and Papua

Additional information
- Accommodation recommendations for different budgets
- Useful contacts and resources for travelers
- Glossary of Indonesian terms

- Maps of major cities and regions
- Conversion charts for currency and measurements

Unveiling the Enchanting Charms of Indonesia: My Unforgettable Vacation in the Archipelago of Wonders

As the plane touched down in Jakarta, I felt a surge of excitement pulsating through my veins. The anticipation of exploring Indonesia, a land brimming with natural beauty, cultural diversity, and warm-hearted people, had been building up for months. Little did I know that this vacation would be an adventure of a lifetime, filled with awe-inspiring moments and indelible memories.

My journey began in the bustling capital city of Jakarta. The vibrant streets, adorned with ornate mosques and towering skyscrapers, beckoned me to immerse myself in its energetic rhythm. I roamed through the historical sites of Kota Tua, marveling at the Dutch colonial architecture and uncovering the stories of Indonesia's past. The National Monument stood tall, symbolizing the nation's independence and offering panoramic views that left me breathless.

From Jakarta, I set my sights on the idyllic island of Bali, affectionately known as the Island of Gods. Bali greeted me with its pristine beaches, where golden sand stretched as far as the eye could see. I surrendered to the rhythmic waves, surfing the crystal-clear waters of Kuta and basking in the sun-kissed paradise of Nusa Dua. Ubud, the cultural heart of Bali, captivated me with its lush rice terraces and enchanting temples. I found myself lost in the mesmerizing dance performances and indulging in the tantalizing flavors of Balinese cuisine.

But my thirst for adventure pushed me further east, to the lesser-explored regions of Flores and Komodo. Trekking through the verdant jungles, I encountered the ancient traditions of the Wae Rebo Village, where cone-shaped houses stood as a testament to a bygone era. Kelimutu National Park, with its mystical three-colored lakes, left me in awe of Mother Nature's artistry. And diving in Komodo National Park, surrounded by vibrant coral reefs and graceful manta rays, felt like entering an underwater wonderland

Throughout my journey, I experienced Indonesia's diverse climates. In Jakarta and Bali, I enjoyed a tropical climate with warm temperatures and high humidity year-round. However, it's worth noting that Bali experiences a wet season from November to March, with increased rainfall. Meanwhile,

Flores and Komodo have a similar climate, with hot and humid conditions, although the rainy season occurs from December to March.

My adventure didn't end there. The allure of Papua beckoned me with its untouched wilderness and breathtaking landscapes. Raja Ampat Islands, with their kaleidoscope of marine life, provided a sanctuary for my soul. Exploring the Baliem Valley, I ventured into the heart of Papua, encountering the traditional Dani tribe and witnessing their rich cultural heritage. Climbing Puncak Jaya, the majestic peak shrouded in clouds, tested my limits and rewarded me with a sense of accomplishment like no other.

As I reflect on my vacation in Indonesia, I am overwhelmed by the memories that will forever hold a special place in my heart. The warm smiles of the Indonesian people, the vibrant colors that painted every corner of the archipelago, and the sense of tranquility I found amidst nature's embrace – all of these experiences have etched themselves into the fabric of my being.

Indonesia, with its diverse landscapes, captivating history, warm hospitality, and varying weather patterns, is a treasure trove waiting to be discovered. My journey through this enchanting archipelago has ignited a lifelong love affair with its beauty and culture. I encourage every wanderlust-filled soul to embark on their own Indonesian adventure, for it promises an extraordinary voyage of discovery, connection, and unforgettable moments that will leave you forever enchanted.

Chapter 1: Introduction to Indonesia

As a frequent visitor, the unique and wonderful land of Indonesia has always inspired me with awe and excitement. Allow me to introduce you to this enthralling land that has a special place in my heart.

Indonesia is the world's biggest archipelago, stretching across the equator in Southeast Asia. It has over 17,000 islands and a diverse range of sceneries, including pristine beaches and blue oceans, lush rainforests, towering volcanoes, and breathtaking rice terraces. I was astounded by the sheer beauty and diversity of its natural beauties as I explored its breadth.

Brief History and Cultural Diversity:

The history of Indonesia is a tapestry woven with influences from numerous civilizations. From the early Hindu and Buddhist dynasties, which left great temples like Borobudur and Prambanan, to the entrance of Islam in the 13th century, which molded the country's cultural and architectural heritage, Indonesia has a rich history. The Dutch colonial era left an everlasting influence on the country as well. Today, Indonesia is proud of its cultural variety, which includes hundreds of ethnic groups with their own languages, traditions, and artistic expressions.

Major Cities and Regions:

As I traveled across Indonesia's major cities, I saw bustling metropolitan hubs that were alive with activity and offered distinct experiences. Jakarta, the vibrant capital, is a cultural mixing pot where traditional marketplaces mingle with modern skyscrapers. Yogyakarta, Java's soul, enchanted me with its royal palaces, batik studios, and vibrant street art scene. Bali, often known as the Island of the Gods, enticed visitors with its spiritual environment, beautiful beaches, and artistic communities. Each city has its own special charm and attractiveness, enticing visitors to immerse themselves in its various flavors.

Climate and Best Time to Visit:

Because Indonesia has a tropical climate, it has warm temperatures all year. However, it is critical to examine the country's two principal seasons: the dry and wet seasons. The dry season, which runs from May to September, is often the ideal time to come because there is less rain and the skies are often clear. This time of year is perfect for exploring beaches, trekking volcanoes, and participating in a variety of outdoor activities. The rainy season, which lasts from October to April, delivers showers but also lush vistas, less tourists, and unique cultural activities.

Travel Tips and Information:

It is critical to be prepared before beginning on your Indonesian vacation. Check that your passport is valid for at least six months after your intended travel date. Check your nationality's visa requirements, since some passengers may be entitled for visa-free entrance, while others may need to obtain a visa on arrival or in advance. Consult your healthcare provider for any essential vaccinations and prescriptions, such as anti-malarial treatments, based on your travel plans.

Indonesia's well-developed transportation infrastructure makes getting around reasonably easy. Domestic flights connect major cities and islands, while railways, buses, and boats give various ways to travel around the country. However, be mindful of potential traffic congestion in cities and plan your journey accordingly.

Remember to respect local customs and traditions when immersing yourself in Indonesia's diverse culture. Indonesians are famed for their gracious hospitality, and a genuine smile and a few words in Bahasa Indonesia can go a long way toward establishing bonds. Engaging with locals, enjoying wonderful street cuisine, and immersing yourself in the country's traditions will certainly enrich your journey.

In this travel handbook, I will share my personal experiences and ideas as we explore Indonesia's hidden treasures, iconic sites, and cultural riches. Prepare to explore the colorful streets.

Discover the historical wonders of Yogyakarta, find peace in the spiritual refuge of Bali, and discover the natural wonders spread over this wonderful archipelago.

Chapter 2: Jakarta Exploration

As someone who has walked the bustling streets of Jakarta, Indonesia's dynamic capital city, I can guarantee you that this metropolis is a fascinating mix of tradition and modernity. Join me as we explore Jakarta's rich tapestry and discover its hidden gems.

Introduction to the Capital City:

Jakarta is Indonesia's beating heart, pulsing with activity and providing a look into the country's complex cultural tapestry. The city's architectural styles and influences range from soaring skyscrapers to historic landmarks.

Top Attractions:

A trip to Jakarta would be incomplete without seeing the city's most famous landmarks. The Monas, or National Monument, stands tall in the city center and offers panoramic views from its observation deck. Adjacent to Monas lies the magnificent Istiqlal Mosque, one of the largest mosques in Southeast Asia, where you can observe the peaceful coexistence of various faiths. The National Museum offers an amazing collection that spans Indonesia's rich cultural heritage for history and art enthusiasts.

Cultural Experiences in Jakarta:

It is essential to immerse oneself in Jakarta's cultural tapestry. Visit the historic Old Town of Kota Tua, whose colonial-era buildings and cobblestone pathways evoke a sense of nostalgia. Explore the area's museums, such as the Jakarta History Museum and the Museum of Fine Arts and Ceramics, to learn more about the city's history. Don't miss the Wayang Museum, which is devoted to the traditional Indonesian art of shadow puppetry and provides fascinating insights into this old storytelling technique.

Shopping and Dining Recommendations:

Jakarta is a haven for both shopaholics and foodies. Indulge in retail therapy in luxury malls such as Plaza Indonesia and Grand Indonesia, which have a mix of international and local designer boutiques. For a more traditional shopping experience, visit Tanah Abang or Pasar Baru, which are noted for their textiles, batik, and street cuisine. When it comes to food, Jakarta has something for everyone. From street food vendors providing delectable foods such as nasi goreng (fried rice) and satay to modern restaurants featuring a fusion of Indonesian and international cuisines, your taste buds will be spoiled for choice.

Practical Tips for Getting Around Jakarta:

Getting around Jakarta may be an adventure in and of itself. To navigate the city's congested streets, take advantage of the city's public transit system, which includes the TransJakarta bus system and the Commuter Line railway. Gojek and Grab are two popular and convenient ride-hailing apps. Be prepared, though, for Jakarta's renowned traffic congestion, particularly during peak hours.

It's critical to be cautious and aware of your surroundings, especially in congested regions. Keep your stuff secure and your personal safety in mind. When visiting holy locations, observe local customs and traditions and dress modestly.

Jakarta, a bustling and ever-changing city, provides a look into Indonesia's past, present, and future.

From cultural encounters to culinary delights, this buzzing capital will captivate and leave you wanting more. Prepare to go on an incredible tour through Jakarta's vibrant streets.

Chapter 3: Bali: The Island of Gods

As soon as I stepped foot on the exotic island of Bali, I was enchanted by its mystical appeal and spiritual aura. Bali, often known as the "Island of Gods," has a vital role in Indonesian culture and has become a popular destination for travelers from all over the world. Join me on a tour through Bali's magnificent landscapes, rich culture, and spiritual treasures.

An Overview of Bali and Its Importance in Indonesian Culture:

Bali is more than just an idyllic island; it is a place where spirituality and tradition coexist with natural beauty. For generations, the Balinese people have preserved their unique cultural history, which is profoundly founded in Hindu beliefs. Bali, with its elaborate temple ceremonies and vibrant festivals, provides a look into a society where spirituality pervades everyday life.

Popular Beach Destinations:

Bali's beautiful beaches are world-renowned for their beauty and surf breaks. Visit the vibrant beach town of Kuta, where beautiful sands and rolling waves draw surfers and sunbathers both. Seminyak provides opulent resorts, trendy beach clubs, and great eating options for a more affluent beach experience. Nusa Dua, with its pristine beaches and world-class resorts, is a peaceful haven for visitors looking to unwind.

Ubud, Bali's Cultural Capital:

Ubud, located in the center of Bali's lush nature, is a refuge for art, spirituality, and traditional craftsmanship. I discovered a lively arts scene as I strolled through its vibrant streets, with galleries displaying beautiful paintings, wood carvings, and traditional crafts. The calm rice terraces of Ubud, such as Tegalalang, provide a look into the island's agricultural history. Don't pass up the chance to experience the healing powers of Ubud's wellness retreats and rejuvenating spa treatments.

Temples and Religious Sites:

Bali is littered with magnificent temples and sacred sites, each with its own distinct tale and architectural splendor. The largest and most prominent Hindu temple complex on the island, Besakih Temple, often known as the "Mother Temple," is poised on the slopes of Mount Agung. Uluwatu Temple, perched on a cliff overlooking the Indian Ocean, provides a stunning backdrop for traditional Kecak dance performances at dusk. Exploring these historic temples connects you to Balinese spirituality and history.

Adventure Activities:

For adrenaline lovers, Bali has a wide selection of adventure activities. The island's world-class surf breaks, such as Uluwatu and Canggu, give the ideal playground for riding the waves, whether you're a beginner or an experienced surfer. In the waters surrounding Nusa Penida and the adjoining islands, divers can explore beautiful coral reefs and encounter marine life. Hiking Mount Batur at sunrise or exploring the lush woods of Bali's interior are memorable experiences for nature enthusiasts.

Balinese Cuisine and Traditional Dance Performances:

Balinese cuisine is a sensory feast. Bali's culinary scene is a blend of Indonesian flavors with local touches, from relishing the fragrant spices of traditional dishes like nasi goreng and satay to sampling the unusual aromas of babi guling (suckling pig). Don't miss out on the chance to see traditional dance performances, such as the hypnotic Barong dance or the exquisite Legong dance, which exhibit the island's rich cultural past through delicate movements and lavish costumes.

The confluence of spirituality, natural beauty, and artistic expression in Bali produces an enthralling environment that stays long after you leave. Bali provides a captivating journey of discovery, whether you want spiritual enlightenment, seaside relaxation, adventurous thrills, or a taste of traditional culture. Prepare to be completely immersed in The Island of Gods' magic.

Chapter 4: Yogyakarta and Central Java

Discovering the Rich History and Heritage of Yogyakarta

When I first arrived in Yogyakarta, I was attracted by the city's rich history and colorful traditions. Yogyakarta, also known as Jogja, is recognized as Java's cultural heart and offers a spectacular voyage through time. Everywhere I turned, I discovered relics of its great history and was struck by the city's profound sense of tradition.

Visiting Borobudur, Prambanan, and Other UNESCO World Heritage Sites

Exploring the majestic Borobudur Temple was one of the highlights of my trip to Yogyakarta. This ancient Buddhist temple, rising magnificently against a backdrop of lush green plains, is a UNESCO World Heritage Site and one of Indonesia's most famous sights. I marveled at the exquisite stone sculptures depicting tales of Buddha's teachings as I climbed the temple's tiers.

Prambanan Temple was another UNESCO World Heritage Site that left me speechless. This massive temple complex, dedicated to Hindu gods, features amazing architecture and beautiful stone reliefs. I couldn't help but feel reverence for Central Java's rich cultural and religious past as I went among the towering spires and explored the countless temples.

The Sultan's Palace (Kraton) and Taman Sari (Water Castle)

I went to the Sultan's Palace, commonly known as Kraton, to learn more about Yogyakarta's regal legacy. This great palace was the residence of Yogyakarta's sultans and is still a cultural and political hub today. I learned about Javanese royal rituals and traditions as I walked through the majestic halls and spacious grounds.

Taman Sari, the picturesque Water Castle, is located adjacent to the Sultan's Palace. This former sultan's private retreat has a complex water system, lush gardens, and a succession of bathing pools. Exploring the underground corridors and vestiges of its former splendor transported me to a time of wealth and tranquillity.

Batik and Wayang Kulit are examples of traditional arts and crafts.

I found the city's rich legacy of arts and crafts while immersing myself in Yogyakarta's cultural scene. Exploring the intricate craft of batik was one of the highlights. I went to a batik workshop and got to watch expert craftspeople methodically apply wax and dyes to create amazing patterns on fabric. I even had the opportunity to try my hand at batik-making, which strengthened my admiration for the art form.

Wayang kulit, or Javanese shadow puppetry, was another traditional art form that captivated me. While seeing a wayang kulit performance, I was captivated by the enchanting sounds of traditional gamelan music as the intricately built puppets came to life. The stories shown in these shadow plays gave an insight into Javanese mythology and cultural narratives.

Outdoor Adventures and Mount Merapi

Yogyakarta provides the ideal combination of cultural exploration and adventure for nature enthusiasts like me. Mount Merapi, just outside the city, beckons with its imposing grandeur. I set out on an adventurous journey up the volcano's slopes, soaking in stunning panoramic views along the way.

Standing at the top, I was rewarded with a sense of success and a breathtaking view stretching as far as the eye could see.

Aside from trekking, Yogyakarta offers adventurous activities such as river rafting, cycling through gorgeous countryside, and finding underground caverns. Each journey allowed me to reconnect with nature and explore the breathtaking landscapes of Central Java.

With their deep-rooted history, rich cultural legacy, and natural beauty, Jakarta and Central Java definitely captured my heart. This region of Indonesia is a treasure trove for travelers seeking an immersive and unforgettable experience, from the awe-inspiring temples to the royal splendors, traditional arts, and adventurous experiences.

Chapter 5: Exploring the Magnificent Komodo Islands

An Overview of Komodo National Park and Its Endangered Wildlife

As soon as I stepped onto the pristine shores of the Komodo Islands, I was captivated by the natural beauty that surrounded me. Komodo National Park, a UNESCO World Heritage Site, is home to a diverse range of animals and stunning scenery. The park is made up of multiple islands, the most well-known of which are Komodo, Rinca, and Padar.

The Komodo dragons, the world's largest living reptiles, are unquestionably the major draw of Komodo National Park. With their archaic appearance, these fearsome creatures walk freely in their natural habitat. During my visit, I had the amazing opportunity to get up close and personal with these gorgeous creatures, escorted by skilled rangers who gave intriguing insights into their behavior and conservation efforts.

Encounters with Komodo Dragons & Guided Tours

I went on organized trips through the harsh terrain of the Komodo and Rinca Islands to see the Komodo dragons in their native habitat. With each stride, I felt a mixture of excitement and awe, well aware of the rare opportunity to see these ancient reptiles in their natural habitat.

I followed well-marked trails with park rangers that guided me to good dragon watching places. I could feel the raw energy emanating from these majestic beasts as I approached. The guides taught us a lot about their behavior, feeding patterns, and the ongoing efforts to conserve their declining population.

Snorkeling and diving in pristine waters

The Komodo Islands are home to not only terrestrial fauna but also a diverse aquatic habitat. It's a snorkeler and diver's paradise, with beautiful coral reefs, abundant marine life, and crystal-clear seas.

I dove into the azure seas, greeted by a kaleidoscope of hues beneath the surface, equipped with snorkeling gear. Tropical fish schools swam around me, and bright coral formations adorned the underwater environment. The sheer beauty and diversity of marine life that thrived in these waters left me speechless.

Komodo National Park provides an even more immersive experience for trained divers. I discovered stunning diving locations filled with marine species as I descended into the depths. Each dive was a fascinating trip that left me in amazement of the underwater beauties of the Komodo Islands, from interactions with beautiful manta rays to the sight of brilliant nudibranchs.

Padar Island and Its Spectacular Viewpoints

A trip to the Komodo Islands would be incomplete without seeing Padar Island. Padar Island, known for its spectacular vistas and panoramic views, is a photographer's dream come true. The island has a distinct geography, with undulating hills and three distinct bays, each with its own beautiful beach.

Hiking to the island's highest point, I was greeted with a stunning view that exceeded my expectations. I gazed in wonder at the steep cliffs, turquoise oceans, and gorgeous beaches that opened before me as the sun painted the sky in orange and pink colors. It was a blissful moment that would live on in my recollection for the rest of my life.

Exploring the Local Villages and Learning About Komodo Culture

Aside from the natural beauty, I was also eager to learn about the Komodo Islands' culture and traditions. I was able to explore the nearby towns, where pleasant locals greeted me with warm grins and open hearts.

I learned about the peasants' way of life by interacting with them, which centered around fishing and making traditional textiles. I observed as expert artisans methodically crafted elaborate designs on their looms, representing the Komodo people's rich cultural past.

As the day came to an end, I had the pleasure of witnessing a traditional dance performance in which locals displayed their elegant movements and colorful clothes. The mesmerizing dancing routines and rhythmic music provided a look into cultural customs passed down through centuries.

With their awe-inspiring animals, enthralling underwater environment, magnificent vistas, and warm hospitality of the local communities, the Komodo Islands left an unforgettable impact on my soul. It was an adventure and a reminder of the value of maintaining the natural treasures that make our world so amazing.

Chapter 6: The Cultural Treasures of Sumatra

Introduction to the Diverse Cultures and Landscapes of Sumatra

I was immediately attracted by Sumatra's varied cultures and different scenery as I began my tour through the island. Sumatra, the world's sixth-largest island, is rich in cultural legacy and natural splendor. Each step showed a new element of this interesting destination, from lush jungles and craggy mountains to calm lakes and lively cities.

Visiting the Bukit Lawang and Ketambe Orangutan Sanctuary

Meeting the sweet and intelligent orangutans was one of the highlights of my trip in Sumatra. I went to the renowned orangutan refuge in Bukit Lawang, which is located in the heart of Gunung Leuser National Park. I set out on a walk through the deep jungle, guided by skilled rangers, anxiously searching for indications of these extraordinary species.

The thrill rose with each step as I caught glimpses of swaying branches and heard distant leaf rustling. Then they appeared, orangutans moving effortlessly through the treetops, their reddish-brown fur standing out against the lush green backdrop. Seeing them in their native environment was an awe-inspiring experience that gave me a strong connection to the natural world.

I continued my journey to Ketambe, another sanctuary buried in Aceh's rough environment. I was able to see orangutans in a more isolated and pristine habitat here. While trekking through the dense rainforest, I marveled at the raw beauty of the surroundings and came upon these beautiful primates in their natural habitat. It was a humbling event that reminded me how important it is to preserve their environment for future generations.

Exploring Samosir Island and Gunung Leuser National Park, both UNESCO World Heritage Sites

Sumatra has two UNESCO World Heritage Sites that should not be missed: Samosir Island and Gunung Leuser National Park. Samosir Island, in the heart of Lake Toba, enchanted me with its tranquil beauty and rich cultural legacy. I explored traditional Batak settlements surrounded by the peaceful waters of the lake, where time appeared to stand still. The peculiar architecture, complex carvings, and ancient stone burials provided views into the Batak people's particular traditions.

I went deep into the lush rainforest of Gunung Leuser National Park, where an unusual ecosystem lives. While hiking through the deep vegetation, I came across a diverse range of flora and fauna, including uncommon species like the Sumatran tiger and Sumatran rhinoceros. The park's untamed environment and pristine splendor left me in awe of nature's power and tenacity.

The Batak Culture and Lake Toba

No trip to Sumatra would be complete without taking in the splendor of Lake Toba, the world's largest volcanic lake. I couldn't help but feel a sense of calm sweep over me as I glanced out over the vast lake, its azure waters stretching to the horizon. I immersed myself in the lively Batak culture by exploring the towns along the lakefront.

I had the pleasure of interacting with the local inhabitants, experiencing their traditional dances, hearing lovely Batak music, and tasting their cuisine. The Batak people's friendliness and hospitality left an indelible impact on me, and I treasured the opportunity to learn about their rituals and way of life.

Traditional Music, Dances, and Culinary Delights

Sumatra's cultural riches were brought to life through traditional dances, music, and culinary pleasures. The mesmerizing performances of the Sigale-gale captivated me.

A Batak dance that tells the legends of ancient spirits. The beautiful motions and vivid costumes transported me to a different planet where old legends were brought to life.

As I listened to the calming melodies played on instruments such as the gondang sabangunan and the taganing, the sounds of traditional Batak music resonated in my ears. The rhythmic beats and lyrical tunes showcased Sumatra's rich musical tradition.

To round off my cultural experience, I sampled the wonderful flavors of Batak cuisine. Every bite and sip was a pleasant study of Sumatra's culinary riches, from saksang (spicy pork) and naniura (raw fish cured in spices) to the distinctly rich aroma of Sumatran coffee.

Sumatra's cultural tapestry, with its varied landscapes, enthralling fauna, and dynamic traditions, has left an indelible imprint on my soul. It was a journey that heightened my senses, broadened my awareness of the world, and instilled a deep appreciation for our planet's astounding diversity.

Chapter 7: Eastern Indonesia: Flores and Beyond

I traveled off the main road to Eastern Indonesia in search of new experiences, and I was rewarded by the beautiful beauty of Flores Island. This undiscovered gem is a haven of rocky coasts, verdant highlands, and quaint traditional towns. Allow me to lead you on a journey across Flores' beautiful landscapes and beyond.

Wae Rebo Village with its customary homes in cone shape:

Immersion in the rich cultural legacy of Wae Rebo Village was one of the highlights of my trip to Flores. This small town in the mountains is well-known for its distinctive cone-shaped thatched roofs on its traditional Mbaru Niang homes. My visit to Wae Rebo was a life-changing experience because of the kind Manggarai residents' friendliness and the tranquil surroundings.

The three lakes in Kelimutu National Park are different colors.

For those who love the outdoors, a trip to Kelimutu National Park is essential. The renowned three-colored lakes can be seen in this park, which is situated near Flores's center. Periodically, the color of these mysterious crater lakes changes, providing a captivating spectacle. I'm in awe of nature's artistic talent as I trek to the lookout, which gives panoramic views of the surrounding mountains and the vivid turquoise, green, and black lakes below.

Beyond Flores, I got the chance to travel to Komodo National Park and dive in its crystal-clear seas to discover its underwater beauties. The abundant marine biodiversity of this UNESCO World Heritage site is well known. I was able to see spectacular Komodo dragons, the biggest lizards on Earth, majestic coral reefs teeming with colorful fish, and graceful manta rays when diving or snorkeling in the pristine waters. It was a strange encounter that gave me priceless memories.

Eastern Indonesia goes beyond Flores and offers a variety of lesser-known islands that are worth exploring, including Sumba, Alor, and Raja Ampat. Sumba won my heart with its own megalithic culture and breathtaking vistas. With its immaculate beaches and abundant marine life, Alor offered a peaceful haven away from the masses. And Raja Ampat in West Papua, a remote paradise, mesmerized me with its picture-perfect islands, azure waters, and top-notch diving locations. Every island in Indonesia has its own unique appeal and provides a window into the country's rich natural and cultural diversity.

Your spirit of adventure will be sparked by the natural wonders and cultural experiences found in Eastern Indonesia. This region begs you to veer off the main track and uncover the true essence of Indonesia's eastern frontier, from the traditional villages of Flores to the underwater wonders of Komodo and the hidden gems of Sumba, Alor, and Raja Ampat. Get ready to be enthralled by Eastern Indonesia's beauty and sincerity.

Chapter 8: The Natural Wonders of Papua

I was astounded by Papua's magnificent natural splendor as soon as I stepped foot on its unspoiled soil. This unspoiled paradise, located in the far eastern region of Indonesia, offers an amazing tapestry of native cultures, wildlife, and landscapes. Join me as we travel through Papua's natural treasures, a place of breathtaking beauty and a thriving cultural history.

Introduction to the Magnificent Natural Beauty of Papua:

Untamed wilderness, luxuriant jungles, soaring mountains, and picturesque islands can be found in Papua. Its scenery are incredibly diverse, which is breathtaking. Papua offers both nature lovers and explorers a playground with its untamed coastlines and rocky mountains. The area is well known for its exceptional biodiversity, which includes a vast number of endemic species and pristine ecosystems just waiting to be discovered.

Islands of Raja Ampat and World-Class Dive Sites:

The Raja Ampat Islands, a marine sanctuary that astounds with its bright coral reefs and rich marine life, are one of Papua's crown jewels. I was welcomed by a kaleidoscope of hues as I dove into the crystal-clear waters: schools of fish, beautiful manta rays, and exotic coral formations. Raja Ampat is a must-visit location for divers and snorkelers who want to experience an underwater world of unmatched beauty.

I traveled inland and came across the alluring Baliem Valley, which is home to the native Dani people, where I was able to observe traditional Dani culture. I observed the Dani people's adaptable way of life and distinctive cultural customs while trekking across the lush slopes. I was in amazement of their rich history as I observed them in their vivid traditional garb, age-old ceremonies, and gorgeous tribal structures.

I was able to gain a comprehensive understanding of Papua's indigenous traditions, their close relationship with nature, and the tenacity of their ancestors' roots through interacting with the Dani tribe.

Climbing Puncak Jaya, Indonesia's Highest Peak:

Puncak Jaya's ascent is the pinnacle of mountaineering difficulty for those seeking the ultimate test of tenacity and resolve. This spectacular peak, with its summit shrouded in mist and ringed by breathtaking glaciers, is Indonesia's highest point. I was pushed to my limits as I began my grueling journey by the rough terrain, difficult weather, and stunning sights. I was rewarded with a sense of victory and astonishment at the breathtaking scene that was unfolding in front of me as I stood atop Puncak Jaya.

Papua is a haven for wildlife aficionados, giving fantastic opportunities for birdwatching and encounters with unusual animals. Wildlife Encounters, including Birdwatching and Orangutan Spotting. The area is home to a diverse range of birds, including the recognizable Birds of Paradise. It was an absolute honor to see these wonderful animals in their natural environment. In addition, I got to see the elusive and endangered orangutans that live in Papua, studying their antics and admiring their grace and intelligence.

Papua is a place of unmatched natural beauty, home to breathtaking landscapes and dynamic civilizations. Papua offers a journey unlike any other, with everything from the undersea wonders of Raja Ampat to the cultural treasures of the Baliem Valley, from the strenuous heights of Puncak Jaya to the enthralling wildlife encounters. Get ready to be amazed and impressed by the untamed environment and untouched beauty of this amazing Indonesian location.

Chapter 9: Practical Information and Travel Tips

Visa Requirements and Entry Restrictions: It's crucial to be informed of the visa requirements and entry restrictions while organizing your trip to Indonesia. I arrived with a tourist visa that permitted me to stay for up to 30 days as a visitor. However, it's important to review the most recent visa guidelines because they may change based on your country of citizenship. While some nations can enter without a visa, others might need one in advance. Make sure to do your homework and get the required visa before you travel.

Travelers are advised to prioritize their health and safety before departing for any country, including Indonesia. I sought advice from my doctor regarding any required immunizations and took preventative measures against frequent diseases like malaria and dengue fever, especially if traveling to isolated locations. Carrying a small first aid kit, applying insect repellent, and drinking plenty of water are all recommended. To guarantee a secure and pleasurable travel, you should also familiarize yourself with regional customs, laws, and emergency contact details.

Indonesian transportation options:

Given the size and variety of the country's landscapes, traveling throughout Indonesia can be an adventure in and of itself. I used a variety of types of transportation during my journey to get around the archipelago. Domestic planes were practical for traveling great distances between islands, while railroads and buses offered more affordable options for shorter trips. Taxis and ride-hailing services were widely accessible in urban areas. It's crucial to schedule your transportation in advance and to take into account variables like cost, convenience, and trip duration.

Money & Budgeting Advice:

Careful planning is necessary to manage your finances when visiting Indonesia. The Indonesian Rupiah (IDR) is the accepted currency, thus I found it useful to bring a variety of cash and have access to ATMs for additional money. Although most larger facilities take credit cards, it's still a good idea to carry cash around for smaller shops and outlying locations. You may make the most of your trip funds by creating a daily budget, studying average expenditures for lodging, meals, and activities, and practicing financial discipline.

Cultural Dos and Don'ts and Etiquette:

In Indonesia, it is crucial to respect local traditions and customs. I made an effort to educate myself on and adhere to cultural etiquette, such as wearing modestly while visiting religious sites, taking off shoes before entering homes or temples, and being aware of appropriate behavior in public places. It's also crucial to understand greetings, gestures, and social standards that are specific to the area. It will substantially improve your contacts with the Indonesian people if you take the time to learn about their culture and to treat them with respect.

Useful Bahasa Indonesian Phrases:

Although English is widely spoken in tourist regions, learning a few fundamental Bahasa Indonesian phrases can go a long way in developing relationships and demonstrating respect for the local way of life. I discovered that knowing phrases like "Selamat pagi," "Terima kasih," and "Permisi" (excuse me) helped me on my journey. In daily encounters, short words like "Tolong" (please), "Ya" (yes), and "Tidak" (no) were also helpful. The

47

villagers were appreciative of my efforts, and it gave my trip adventure a greater sense of authenticity.

You'll be better prepared to traverse Indonesia, guarantee your safety and well-being, and develop deep relationships with the local culture by becoming familiar with useful facts and travel advice. Accept the challenge and get ready for an unforgettable trip across the captivating wonders of this magnificent nation.

Chapter 10: Sample Itineraries

Bali Highlights & Must-See Places in One Week

I spent a week traveling in Bali and found a treasure trove of stunning natural scenery, fascinating cultural sites, and picture-perfect beaches. To help you make the most of your stay on the Island of Gods, here is an example itinerary:

- Day 1: Departure for Bali and Tour of Ubud
- Day 2: Seminyak Beach Day and Tanah Lot Temple Sunset
- Day 3: Beautiful Drive to Tegalalang's Rice Terraces and Tirta Empul Temple
- Day 4: Visiting Uluwatu Temples and Observing a Kecak Dance Performance
- Day 5 of the Ubud Adventure: Tegenungan Waterfall, Monkey Forest, and Ubud Art Market Island-hopping on Day 6 to Nusa Lembongan and Nusa Penida
- Day 7: Relaxation Day: Nusa Dua Beach Time and Goodbye to Bali

Discovering Jakarta, Yogyakarta, and Mount Bromo in Two Weeks in Java

I was able to explore Java's fascinating history, dynamic culture, and breathtaking scenery by setting out on a two-week journey throughout the island. Discover Java's top attractions by following this suggested itinerary:

- Day 1-3: Visiting the National Monument, Istiqlal Mosque, and Kota Tua as you explore Jakarta
- Days 4–7 of Yogyakarta's Cultural Immersion Tour: Borobudur Temple, Prambanan Temple, and Kraton Palace
- Day 8–10: Sunrise Trek, Savanna, and Whispering Sands on Mount Bromo
- Day 11–12: Surabaya City Tour and Pasar Atom Shopping
- Day 13–14: Leisure in Malang and Goodbye, Java

Off-the-Beaten-Path Adventure: Raja Ampat, Flores, and Komodo

Exploring Flores, Komodo, and Raja Ampat offers a special fusion of natural beauties and cultural experiences for anyone looking for a really exciting journey. Here is an example itinerary to encourage your sense of adventure:

- Day 1-3: Discovering Flores' Beauty: Komodo National Park, Wae Rebo Village, and Labuan Bajo
- Day 4-6: Manta Point, Pink Beach, and Rinca Island diving in Komodo
- Day 7–10 of the Raja Ampat Expedition: Misool, Wayag, and Gam Island Exploration
- Day 11–12: Cultural Immersion and City Tour in Sorong
- Day 13: Rest in Papua's Baliem Valley
- Day 14: Bid Papua adieu and head home with priceless memories

Suitable for Families: Bali and Lombok

Family vacations offer the chance to create cherished memories and share experiences. Here is a typical schedule for a trip to Bali and Lombok that is suitable for families:

Family-friendly activities in Bali include Waterbom Bali, Bali Safari and Marine Park, and Tanjung Benoa Water Sports. Cultural activities in Ubud include a visit to a monkey forest, a waterfall, and a Balinese dance performance.

- Day 8–12: Gili Islands, Mount Rinjani National Park, and Kuta Beach are part of an island getaway to Lombok.
- Day 13: Travel back to Bali and unwind at Nusa Dua
- Day 14: Saying goodbye to Indonesia with hearts that are joyful and united

Itinerary with a focus on nature and wildlife: Sumatra and Papua

Sumatra and Papua provide unmatched interactions with diverse flora and fauna for nature lovers and wildlife aficionados. Use this sample itinerary as a guide.

Take in all that nature has to offer:

- Day 1-3: Visiting the UNESCO-listed Gunung Leuser National Park and Medan
- Day 4–7: Bukit Lawang Wildlife Encounters: Jungle Adventures and Orangutan Trekking

- Day 8–10: Samosir Island and Traditional Batak Culture on the Way to Lake Toba
- Day 11–14: Papua's Natural Wonders: Puncak Jaya Trek, Raja Ampat, and Baliem Valley

These sample itineraries give you a taste of the variety of experiences Indonesia has to offer. By altering them to fit your choices, you can travel according to your unique interests and aspirations. Prepare to make lasting experiences in the alluring Indonesian archipelago.

Additional information

Accommodation Recommendations for Different Budgets

Budget: Hostels, guesthouses, and homestays are a great option for budget travelers. These accommodations are typically clean and comfortable, and they offer a variety of amenities, such as shared bathrooms, free Wi-Fi, and breakfast.

Hostels in Indonesia

Mid-range: Hotels and resorts are a good option for travelers who want a bit more comfort and privacy. These accommodations typically offer private bathrooms, air conditioning, and other amenities.

Luxury: Luxury hotels and villas offer the best in terms of comfort and amenities. These accommodations typically have private pools, butler service, and other high-end features.

Luxury hotels in Indonesia

Luxury villas in Indonesia

Useful Contacts and Resources for Travelers

Tourism board: The Indonesian Tourism Board (ITB) is a good resource for information on travel to Indonesia. The ITB website has a wealth of information on destinations, transportation, accommodation, and other travel-related topics.

Embassy or consulate: If you are a citizen of a foreign country, you should contact your embassy or consulate in Indonesia for information on visa requirements, safety and security, and other important travel matters.

Local hospitals and clinics: It is a good idea to have the contact information for local hospitals and clinics in case of an emergency. You can find this information in your hotel or hostel, or you can contact the ITB website.

Currency exchange: The official currency of Indonesia is the Indonesian Rupiah (IDR). You can exchange your currency for IDR at banks, currency exchange bureaus, and some hotels.

Transportation: There are a variety of transportation options available in Indonesia, including airplanes, trains, buses, taxis, and motorbikes. The best way to get around will depend on your destination and budget.

Visas: Citizens of most countries need a visa to enter Indonesia. You can apply for a visa at your nearest Indonesian embassy or consulate.

Safety and security: Indonesia is generally a safe country to travel to, but it is important to be aware of your surroundings and take precautions against petty theft and other crimes. You should also be aware of the risk of terrorism, especially in certain parts of the country.

Glossary of Indonesian Terms

Selamat datang: Welcome

Terima kasih: Thank you

Permisi: Excuse me

Tolong: Please

Bahasa Indonesia: The Indonesian language

Rumah makan: Restaurant

Rumah makan in Indonesian

Warung: Small restaurant or food stall

Image of Warung in Indonesian

Image of Hotel in Indonesian
Losmen: Guesthouse

Losmen in Indonesian

Sepeda motor: Motorbike

Sepeda motor in Indonesian

Taksi: Taxi

Taxi in Indonesian

Becak: Three-wheeled bicycle rickshaw

Becak in Indonesian

Ojek: Motorcycle taxi

Ojek in Indonesian

Maps of Major Cities and Regions

Jakarta: The capital of Indonesia

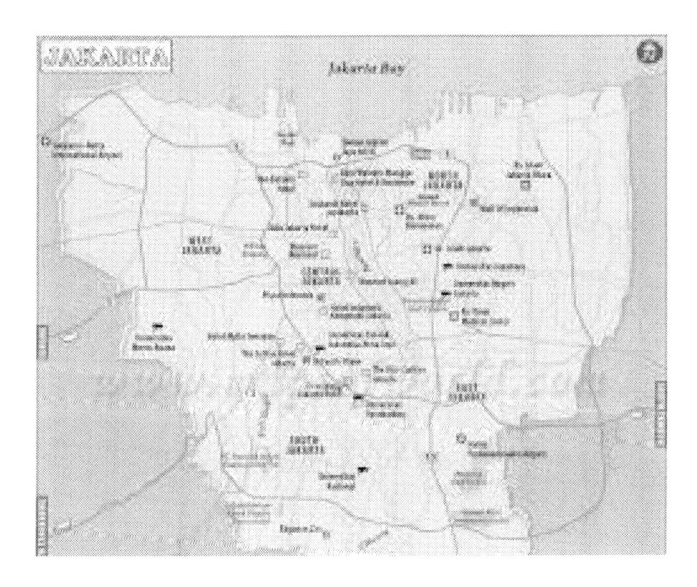

Jakarta map

Yogyakarta: A city in central Java known for its historical and cultural attractions

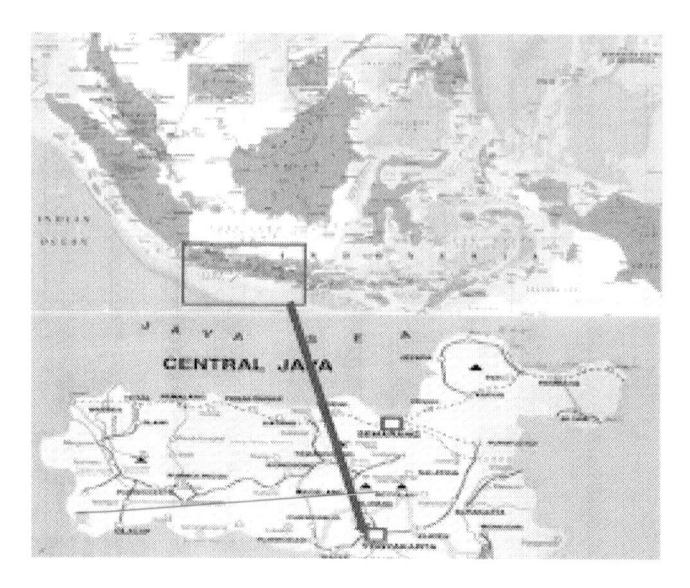

Yogyakarta map

Bali: An island in eastern Indonesia known for its beaches, resorts, and cultural attractions

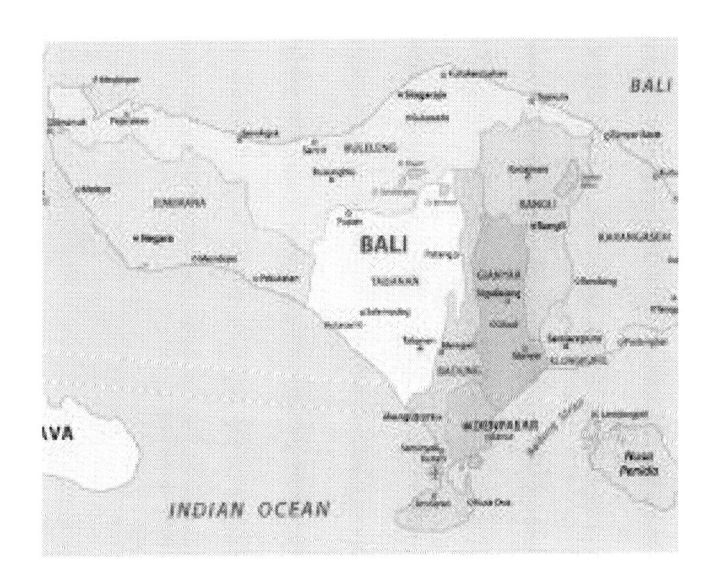

Bali map

Lombok: An island east of Bali known for its beaches and natural beauty

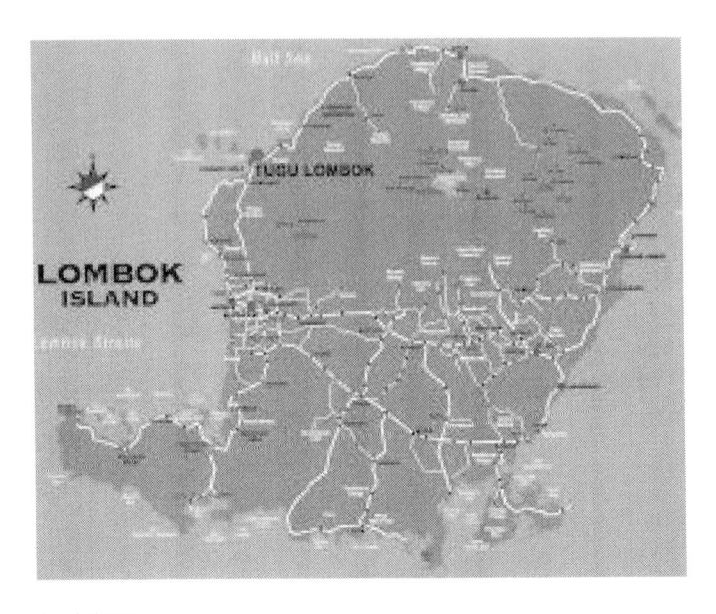

Lombok map

Komodo: An island in eastern Indonesia known for its Komodo dragons

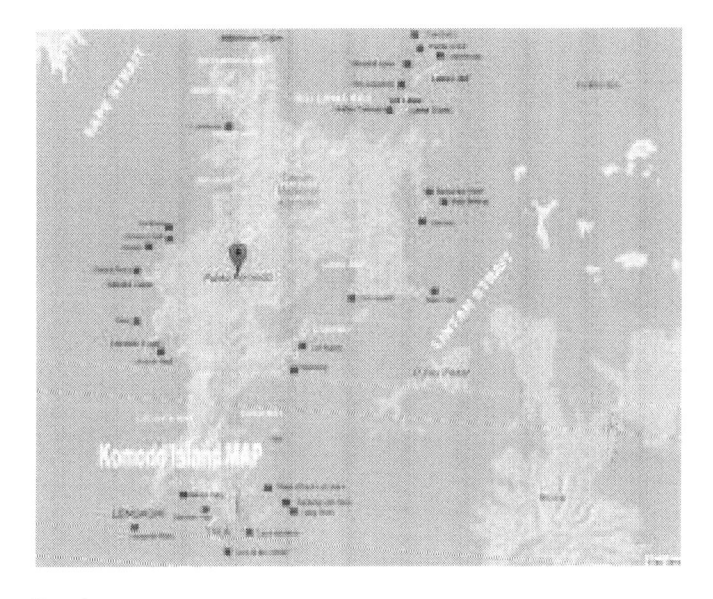

Komodo map

Conversion Charts for Currency and Measurements

Currency: The official currency of Indonesia is the Indonesian Rupiah (IDR).

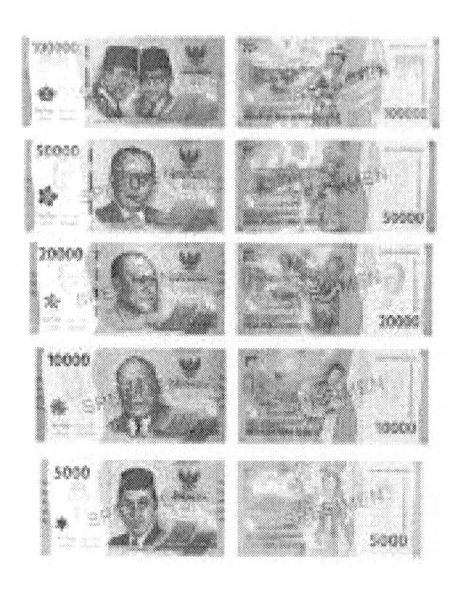

Indonesian Rupiah (IDR) currencies

Measurements: The official measurement system in Indonesia is the metric system.

IndonesiaTourism: https://www.indonesia.travel/en/

The Culture Trip: Indonesia: https://theculturetrip.com/asia/indonesia/

Lonely Planet: Indonesia: https://www.lonelyplanet.com/indonesia/

Wikitravel: Indonesia: https://wikitravel.org/en/Indonesia

THE END

Made in the USA
Coppell, TX
19 August 2024